SONATA I IN F

Tuba and Piano

BENEDETTO MARCELLO (1686-1739)
*Transcribed by Donald C. Little
and Richard B. Nelson*

Sonata No. I

(IN F MAJOR)

BY

Benedetto Marcello

FOR

Tuba and Keyboard

ARRANGED BY

Donald C. Little and Richard B. Nelson

SONATA IN IN F

Tuba

BENEDETTO MARCELLO (1686-1739)
*Transcribed by Donald C. Little
and Richard B. Nelson*

4

6

Allegro ♩=92–102

8